MW00669069

THE SECOND BOOK OF MEZZO-SOPRANO/ALTO SOLOS

PART II

compiled by Joan Frey Boytim

ISBN 978-0-634-06568-2

G. SCHIRMER, *Inc.*

DISTRIBUTED BY

7777 W. BLUEMOUND RD. P.O. BOX 13819 MILWAUKEE, WI 53213

Copyright © 2004 by G. Schirmer, Inc. (ASCAP) New York, NY
International Copyright Secured. All Rights Reserved.
**Warning: Unauthorized reproduction of this publication is
prohibited by Federal law and subject to criminal prosecution.**

www.schirmer.com
www.halleonard.com

PREFACE

Many teachers have expressed the desire to have a second volume to complement *The Second Book of Solos* series for those high school and college students studying more advanced student literature. In my studio, I have found that students using the four volumes of *Easy Songs for Beginning Singers* in seventh and eighth grades move very easily into *The First Book of Solos* and *The First Book of Solos–Part II* in ninth and tenth grades. Several of my students have moved into *The Second Book of Solos* as early as eleventh grade. They would find the variety of *The Second Book of Solos–Part II* a welcome addition to their repertoire for eleventh and twelfth grades. With many of today's college freshmen using *The First Book of Solos* and *The First Book of Solos–Part II*, *The Second Book of Solos* and this new *Part II* will prove to be a great launching pad of further new repertoire for freshman and sophomores.

The songs introduced in this volume are on comparable levels of sophistication and musical difficulty with those found in *The Second Book of Solos*, and could be used at the same time to provide more variety of repertoire. Each voice volume has representative English, American, Russian, Italian, German, French, sacred, oratorio, and Gilbert and Sullivan selections not used previously in any of my other anthologies. There are a number of out-of-print songs which deserved to be reissued, and quite a number of unfamiliar songs which should find a place in student repertoire.

In these volumes we have been able to include pieces from more contemporary composers such as Barber, Bax, Bowles, Chanler, Duke, Dougherty, Hoiby, Ives, Griffes, Gurney, Lekberg, Sacco, Thomson, and Warlock. The relatively unknown French composer, Félix Fourdrain, is represented in three of the four volumes. These songs, as well as other unfamiliar French mélodies, have only been available in single sheet form and have never before had English singing translations. For these songs, a life-long vocal accompanist and retired French professor, Harry Goldby, has made very singable texts which relate very closely to the original poems. My excitement mounts when I think of those students who will enjoy learning many of these more unfamiliar songs, as well as those songs that have been difficult to find.

This set of four books will conclude the more advanced portion of this 16 volume basic series of teaching material for soprano, mezzo-soprano/alto, tenor, and baritone/bass (the four volumes of *The First Book of Solos*, the four volumes of *The First Book of Solos–Part II*, the four volumes of *The Second Book of Solos*, and now the four volumes of *The Second Book of Solos–Part II*). There are 528 different songs included in the 16 volumes, with an average of 132 songs of all varieties carefully chosen for content and suitability for each voice part. I only wish I had had all of these books for teaching when my studio began over 45 years ago!

Joan Frey Boytim
May, 2004

CONTENTS

AFFANNI DEL PENSIER

(O Agonies of Thought)

English version by Dr. Theodore Baker

George Frideric Handel
(1685-1759)

fan - ni del__ pen - sier, un sol mo - men - to

ag - o - nies__ of thought, one mo - ment on - ly

Copyright, 1894, by G. Schirmer, Inc.
Copyright renewal assigned, 1926, to G. Schirmer, Inc.

un sol____ mo - men - to   da - te - mi pa - ce al-
one mo - ment on - ly   leave me in peace a-

men,____   e poi tor - na - te,   tor - na - - -
gain,____   then turn   and   rend me,   one mo - - -

te,____   e poi tor - na - te;   Af - fan - ni del__ pen - sier,
ment, then turn   and rend me;   O   ag - o - nies__ of thought,

da - te - mi pa - ce almen,   e poi tor - na - - te,   e poi,____
leave me in peace a - gain   one moment on - ly, and then,____

e   po - i   tor - na - te.

then turn_____ and   rend_____ me.

AH, LOVE BUT A DAY!

Robert Browning

Amy Beach
(1867-1944)

Lento con molto espressione

Ah, Love, but a day, And the world has changed! Ah, Love, but a day, And the world has

Copyright © 2004 by G. Schirmer, Inc. (ASCAP) New York, NY
International Copyright Secured. All Rights Reserved.

ritenuto molto   a tempo

but _ a day, And the world has changed! _____

dim.   pp

Look   in __ my eyes! _____ Wilt

legatissimo

with pedal

thou _____ change too?

Look in ___ my eyes! _____ Wilt thou _____ change too? _____ Should I fear _____ sur - prise? Shall I find aught new In the old _____ and dear, In the good and true _____

cresc. e agitato

accel.

ALL MEIN GEDANKEN
(All The Fond Thoughts)

Felix Dahn
English version by John Bernhoff

Richard Strauss
(1864-1949)

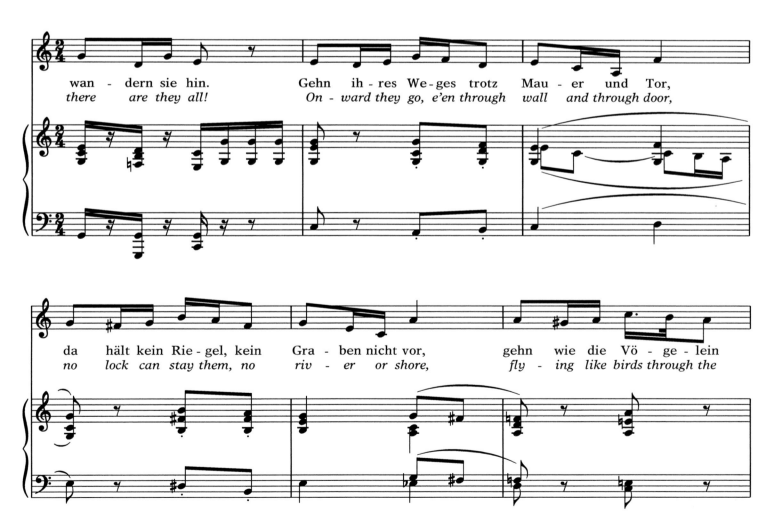

Copyright © 2004 by G. Schirmer, Inc. (ASCAP) New York, NY
International Copyright Secured. All Rights Reserved.

ALLERSEELEN
(All Soul's Day)

Hermann von Gilm

English version by Florence Easton

Richard Strauss
(1864-1949)

Copyright © 1951 by G. Schirmer, Inc. (ASCAP) New York, NY
International Copyright Secured. All Rights Reserved.

einst im Mai.
once in May.

Gib mir die Hand, dass
Give me your hand, in

ich sie heim-lich drük - ke,
se - cret I'll ca - ress it.

und wenn man's sieht,
Should oth - ers see,

mir ist es ei - ner-lei,
I'll care not what they say.

gib mir nur ei - nen
A-gain en-thrall me

dei - ner süs - sen Blik - ke, wie einst im
with your glance so ten - der, As once in

Mai.
May.

Es blüht und duf - tet heut' auf je - dem
To - day on ev - 'ry grave the flow'rs are

Gra- be, ein Tag im Jahr ist ja den To- ten frei, komm an mein
bloom- ing, One day each year all who have died are free, Come to my

Herz, _____ dass ich dich wie- der ha- be, wie einst im
heart, _____ that I a- gain may hold you, As once in

Mai,
May,
wie einst im
as once in

Mai.
May.

AS THOU WILT, FATHER

from *Gethsemane*

C. Lee Williams
(1853-1935)

Andante.

O gra-cious Fa-ther, wise and kind, Thou know-est what is best,

And oft through storms Thy chil-dren find The ha-ven of Thy rest, the

ha-ven of Thy rest. Lord, grant me, when earth's troubles cease,

Adagio.

To en-ter Thine e-ter-nal peace.

A - - men.

AU JARDIN DE MON PÈRE
(In My Dear Father's Garden)

English version by Harry Goldby

Pauline Viardot
(1821-1910)

Copyright © 2004 by G. Schirmer, Inc. (ASCAP) New York, NY
International Copyright Secured. All Rights Reserved.

Mi - gnon - - ne, Ay - mez -
My dar - - ling, love me,

moy! _____
please! _____

Trois jeu - nes de - moi - sel - les L'y si vont om - brai -
Three young and pret - ty maid - ens like to rest in its

ger; _____
shade; _____

Trois jeu - nes gen - tils -
Three young and hand - some

le Et la pri - ay de m'ai - mer! _____
and en - treat - ed her to love me! _____

l.h.

Mon père est dans sa cham - bre,
My fa - ther's in his cham - ber

p

Al - lez lui de - man - der! _____
Go there and ask him now! _____

pp

pp

Ay - mez - moy, ma mi - gnon - ne, Ay - mez -
Love me please, pret - ty maid - en, come with

pp

moi sans dan - ger. _____ Mon père est dans sa cham - bre, Al -
me have no fear. _____ My fa - ther's in his cham - ber, go

p

rit.

lez luy de - man - der... Et s'il en est con - tent, et
there and ask him now. And if he is con - tent, and

a tempo
f *decisively*

s'il en est con - tent, Et s'il en est con - tent, Je me veux ac - cor -
if he is well pleased, and if he is con - tent, then I too shall a -

der! _____
gree! _____

f

AVRIL
(April)

Rémy Belleau

Léo Delibes
(1836-1891)

Copyright © 2004 by G. Schirmer, Inc. (ASCAP) New York, NY
International Copyright Secured. All Rights Reserved.

cresc.

cieux, Sen - tent l'o - deur de la plai - ne, sen - tent l'o -
love, Come o'er the plain to us blow - ing, Come o'er the

un poco allarg. a tempo

deur de la plai - ne. _____
plain to us blow - ing. _____

colla voce

mf

C'est
The

p

core

z ruh

toi, cour - tois et gen - til, Qui d'e - xil ___ Re - ti - res ces
swal - lows thou one and all, Dost re - call ___ From climes they sought,

THE AWAKENING

Edward Teschemacher

Eric Coates
(1886-1957)

Copyright © 2004 by G. Schirmer, Inc. (ASCAP) New York, NY
International Copyright Secured. All Rights Reserved.

And yet, some-how, when you had passed a-

far, New sun-beams filled the day, new

stars the night.

When first you spoke to me,

I on - ly deemed _____ Your voice, like

ma - ny o - ther voi - - - ces, sweet, _____

And yet as I went sing - ing on my way, _____

New flow - ers seemed to wake a - round my feet.

BEFORE MY WINDOW

Sergei Rachmaninoff
(1873-1943)

English version by Henry G. Chapman

Lento ed un poco pensieroso

Be - fore my win - dow blows a scent - ed al - der

tree, Who wears with se - rious grace his fes - tal robe of

flow - ers; Some per - fumed branch - es,

with pedal

poco cresc.

la melodia ben portando ed espressivo

Copyright © 2004 by G. Schirmer, Inc. (ASCAP) New York, NY
International Copyright Secured. All Rights Reserved.

CHANSON TRISTE
(A Song of Sorrow)

Jean Lahor
English version by M. Louise Baum

Henri Duparc
(1844-1933)

Dans le calme ai - mant
Yearns for sweet re - pose

de tes bras!
in thine arms?

Tu prendras ma tê - te ma -
Thou wilt lay my head, dull with

CHERRY VALLEY

Joseph Campbell

Roger Quilter
(1877-1953)

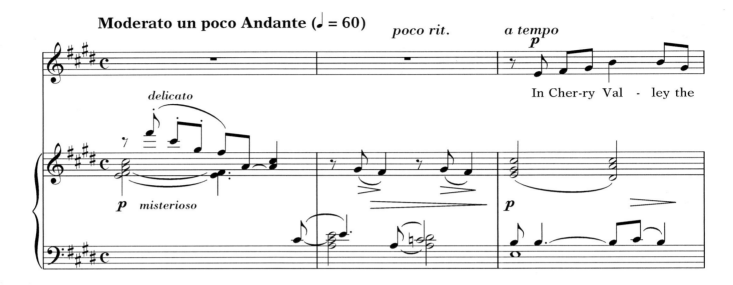

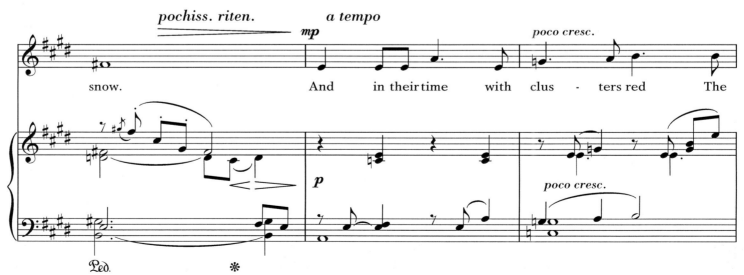

Copyright © 2004 by G. Schirmer, Inc. (ASCAP) New York, NY
International Copyright Secured. All Rights Reserved.

pet - al trem-bles to the grass,_____ The feet of fai - ries

pass_____ and pass._____

In Cher-ry Val - ley the cher-ries blow; The val-ley paths are white as snow;

white as snow._____

DU MEINES HERZENS KRÖNELEIN
(Pride of My Heart)

Felix Dahn
English version by John Bernhoff

Richard Strauss
(1864-1949)

Du meines Her - zens Krö - ne-lein, du bist von laut' - rem
Pride of my heart, its crown, its joy, thou art a gold - en

Gol - de, wenn an - de - re da - ne - ben sein, dann
trea - sure, com-pared to thee, all is al - loy: none

bist du erst viel hol - de. Die an - dern tun so gern ge -
can thy vir - tues mea - sure. While o - thers boast with words of

Copyright © 2004 by G. Schirmer, Inc. (ASCAP) New York, NY
International Copyright Secured. All Rights Reserved.

Au - gen kunst bist wert an al - len Or - ten.
glance or smile, art sought for in all pla - ces.

Du bist als wie die Ros' im Wald, sie weiß nichts_____ von ih-rer
Thou art like to the wood - land rose that knows_____ nought of its

Blü - te, doch je - dem, der vor - ü - ber - wallt, er -
beaut - y, but charms each wand - 'rer pass - ing by with

freut_____ sie das Ge - mü - te.
fra - grance sweet and beau - ty.

DU RING AN MEINEM FINGER

Adelbert von Chamisso
English version by Frederic Field Bullard

Robert Schumann
(1810-1856)

Copyright © 2004 by G. Schirmer, Inc. (ASCAP) New York, NY
International Copyright Secured. All Rights Reserved

Ring an mei-nem Fin - ger, mein_ gol - de-nes Rin - ge-
ring up-on my fin - ger, My_ dear lit-tle ring of

lein, ich_ drü - cke dich fromm an die Lip - pen, dich
gold, I_ press thee de-vot - ed-ly to my lips, De -

fromm an die Lip-pen, an das Her - ze mein.
vot - ed-ly now up-on my heart I hold.

ET EXULTAVIT SPIRITUS MEUS
(And My Spirit Hath Rejoiced)
from *Magnificant*

Johann Sebastian Bach
(1685-1750)

Et ex- ul - ta - vit spi - ri - tus me - us,
And__ my spir - it hath__ re - joic - ed,

et ex - ri - ta - vit spi - ri - tus me - us,
and__ my spir - it hath__ re - joic - ed,

IMMER LEISER WIRD MEIN SCHLUMMER
(Ever Gentler Grows My Slumber)

Hermann Lingg

Johannes Brahms
(1833-1897)

Im - mer lei - ser wird mein Schlum - mer,
Ev - er gen - tler grows my slum - ber,

nur wie Schlei - er liegt mein Kum - mer zit - ternd ü - ber
Veil - like now the griefs I num - ber Hov - er o - ver

mir, ___ ü - ber mir. ___ Oft im
me, ___ o - ver me; ___ In my

Ja, ich wer - de ster - ben müs - sen,
Death for me I know that this ___ is,

ei - ne And - re wirst du küs - sen,
Some - one else will have thy kiss - es

wenn ich bleich und kalt, ___ bleich ___ und
When I'm cold and dumb, ___ cold ___ and

kalt. ___
dumb. ___

Eh' die Mai - en - lüf - te weh'n, eh' die
Once, be - fore the A - pril rain, Ere the

dim.

L'HEURE EXQUISE
(The Exquisite Time)

Paul Verlaine
English version by Theodore Baker

Lady Dean Paul Poldowski
(Irena Regina Wieniawski)
(1880-1932)

Copyright © 2004 by G. Schirmer, Inc. (ASCAP) New York, NY
International Copyright Secured. All Rights Reserved.

LORD, LEAD ME IN THY RIGHTEOUSNESS

Luigi Cherubini
(1760-1842)

Copyright © 2004 by G. Schirmer, Inc. (ASCAP) New York, NY
International Copyright Secured. All Rights Reserved.

plain be-fore my face, Thy way plain be - fore my

face. O hear me when I call to Thee, and go not far a -

way from me. Lord, lead me in Thy right - eous-ness,

O hear me when I call to Thee,

call to Thee, and go not far a - way from me, make Thy way

plain _____ be - fore my face, and

go _____ not far, not ___ far _____ from

me, make Thy way plain _____ be - fore my face.

Lord, _____ lead me in Thy right - eous-ness,

p

O _____ hear me when I call to Thee,

O _____ lead _____ me,

make   Thy   way

LORD TO THEE, EACH NIGHT AND DAY

from *Theodora*

George Frederic Handel
(1685-1759)

Lord, to Thee, each night and day, Strong in hope we

sing and pray strong in hope we sing and pray, each night and

sing___ and pray, we sing and pray, strong in hope___ we sing___ and

pray.

Allegro moderato. (♩= 92)

Though con-vul-sive rocks the ground, And Thy thunders roll a -

round, and Thy thunders roll a - round,

Still to Thee, each night and

day, still to Thee we sing and pray, though con-vul-sive rocks the ground, and Thy thunders roll a-round, still to Thee we sing and pray.

Dal Segno al Fine.

LUNGI DA TE

Giovanni Bononcini
(1670-1747)

Lungi da te ben mio
Morto al piacer son io,
Son vivo al mio dolor,

Far away from you, my love,
I am dead to pleasure,
Alive to every pain.

E pur la speme io sento
Dirmi: Sarai contento, se torni a riveder
Sull' ali del pensier

Yet the voice of hope is saying
Turn and look again –
In the magic cup of memory,

L'oggetto del tuo amor.

You will see your love.

DIE MAINACHT
(The May Night)

Ludwig Hölty
English version by Paul England

Johannes Brahms
(1833-1897)

Sehr langsam und ausdrucksvoll
Largo ed expressivo

Wann der sil - ber-ne
When the sil - ver - y

Mond durch die Ge-sträu - che blinkt, und sein schlum-mern-des
moon shines through the wo - ven boughs, Bath - ing mead - ow and

Licht ü - ber den Ra - sen streut, und die Nach - ti - gall
lawn all in a slumb - 'rous light, While the night - in-gale

Copyright © 1937 by G. Schirmer, Inc. (ASCAP) New York, NY
International Copyright Secured. All Rights Reserved.

MON JARDIN
(My Garden)

André Alexandre
English version by Harry Goldby

Félix Fourdrain
(1880-1923)

Copyright © 2004 by G. Schirmer, Inc. (ASCAP) New York, NY
International Copyright Secured. All Rights Reserved.

NEBBIE
(Mists)

Ada Negri
English version by Lorraine Noel Finley

Ottorino Respighi
(1879-1936)

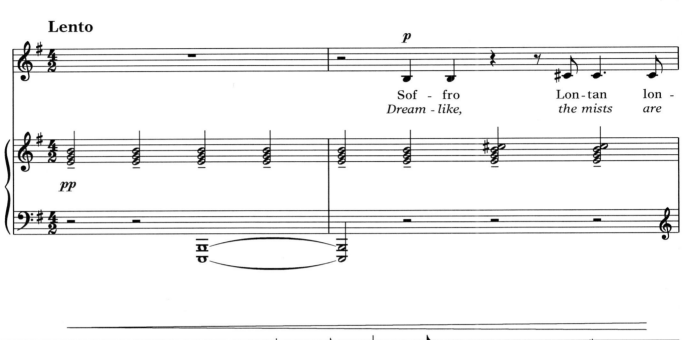

Copyright © 1939 by G. Schirmer, Inc. (ASCAP) New York, NY
International Copyright Secured. All Rights Reserved.

QUI SEDES
(Who Sittest?)
from *Gloria*

Antonio Vivaldi
(1678-1741)

Copyright © 2004 by G. Schirmer, Inc. (ASCAP) New York, NY
International Copyright Secured. All Rights Reserved.

cresc.

f

mi - se - re - re, mi - se - re - re ____
Lord, *have* *mer* - *cy,* *mer* - *cy,* ____ *Lord,* *up* -

____ no - bis.
- *on* *us.*

f

mi - se - re - re, mi - se - re - re, mi - se -
Lord, have mer - cy, Lord, have mer - cy, mer - cy,

re - re _____ no - bis.
Lord, up - on us.

senza rit.

SE TU DELLA MIA MORTE
(Would'st Thou the Boast of Ending)

English version by Dr. Theodore Baker

Alessandro Scarlatti
(1660-1725)

Copyright, 1894, by G. Schirmer, Inc.
Copyright renewal assigned, 1926, to G. Schirmer, Inc.

SERENITY

John Greenleaf Whittier

Charles Ives
(1874-1954)

Copyright © 1942 (Renewed) by Associated Music Publishers, Inc. (BMI), New York, NY.
International Copyright Secured. All Rights Reserved.

SONG OF DEVOTION

Adapted from
Philippians 1:3-11

John Ness Beck
(1930-1987)

Copyright © 1968 by G. Schirmer, Inc. (ASCAP) New York, NY
International Copyright Secured. All Rights Reserved.

SONG OF THE OPEN

Jessica Hawley Lowell

Frank La Forge
(1879-1953)

Copyright © 2004 by G. Schirmer, Inc. (ASCAP) New York, NY
International Copyright Secured. All Rights Reserved.

play _____ Of the foam - ing spray, _____ Where

Animato

mad waves romp on the long low beach? To

broadly

stand just out of their fran - tic reach, My

hair blown free and the breath of me Caught

LA SPERANZA È GIUNTA
(Spring)
from *Otho*

English version by Arthur Somervell

George Frideric Handel
(1685-1759)

La spe-ran-za è giun-ta in por-to
Spring is com-ing With sun and shower and blos-som.

Optional abbreviated introduction, cut to **.

Copyright © 2004 by G. Schirmer, Inc. (ASCAP) New York, NY
International Copyright Secured. All Rights Reserved.

nè   sa più di ___ che   te - me   -   re Se   tran-quil - lo ___
Lads   *are court*   -   *ing,* _ *Lambs*   *are sport* - *ing, Na*   -   *ture wakes* _ *to the*

ve   -   de il mar.   Se   tran-quil - lo   ve - de il mar ___
hum _ *of the bee.*   *Birds*   *are sing*   -   *ing,*   *I hear them sing*   -   *ing*

Se _ tran-quil - lo _ ve - de il mar.
Their car - ols ring   -   *ing from ev*   -   *'ry tree.*

Nè   sa   più __   di
Birds   are sing-ing   I

che __ te - me - re ____ Se   tran-quil - lo   ve - de il mar.
hear _____   their_ car - ols ring-ing from ev - 'ry tree.

TEARS

Wang Seng-Ju
(6th Century)

Charles T. Griffes
(1884-1920)

Copyright, 1917, by G. Schirmer, Inc.
Copyright renewal assigned, 1945, to G. Schirmer, Inc.

THE TWENTY-THIRD PSALM

Albert Hay Malotte
(1865-1924)

Copyright © 1937 by G. Schirmer, Inc. (ASCAP) New York, NY
International Copyright Secured. All Rights Reserved.

WHEN A MERRY MAIDEN MARRIES

from *The Gondoliers*

W.S. Gilbert

Arthur Sullivan
(1842-1900)

Allegro grazioso

When a mer-ry mai-den mar - ries,

Sor - row goes and pleas-ure tar - ries, Ev - 'ry sound be-comes a

song, All is right and noth-ing's wrong! From to - day and ev - er

Copyright © 2004 by G. Schirmer, Inc. (ASCAP) New York, NY
International Copyright Secured. All Rights Reserved.

af - ter   Let our tears be tears of   laugh - ter.   Ev -'ry sigh that finds a

vent   Be a   sigh of sweet   con - tent!   When you mar-ry, mer-ry

rall.   *a tempo sostenuto*

maid - en,   Then the air with love is   lad - en;   Ev -'ry flow'r   is   a

rose, Ev - 'ry goose be-comes a swan,   Ev -'ry kind of trou - ble

goes Where the last year's snows have gone! Sun-light takes the place of

shade ___ When you mar-ry, mer-ry maid. ___ When a mer-ry maid-en

mar - ries, Sor - row goes and pleas-ure tar - ries; Ev - 'ry sound be-comes a

song, All is right and noth - ing's wrong!

When a mer-ry maid-en mar - ries

Sor-row goes and pleas-ure tar - ries; Ev-'ry sound be-comes a song All is

right and noth-ing's wrong. Gnaw-ing Care and ach-ing Sor - row

Get ye gone un-til to - mor - row; Jeal-ous-ies in grim ar - ray, Ye are

things of yes - ter - day! When you mar-ry mer-ry maid - en,

rall.

Then the air with joy is lad - en; All the cor-ners of the earth Ring with

a tempo, sostenuto

mu - sic sweet-ly played, Wor-ry is mel-o - dious mirth, Grief is

joy in mas-que - rade; Sul-len night is laugh-ing day ____

WHEN FREDERIC WAS A LITTLE LAD

from *The Pirates of Penzance*

W.S. Gilbert

Arthur Sullivan
(1842-1900)

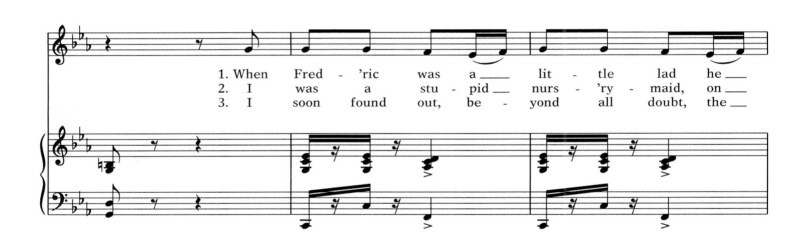

1. When Fred - 'ric was a ___ lit - tle lad he ___
2. I was a stu - pid ___ nurs - 'ry - maid, on ___
3. I soon found out, be - yond all doubt, the ___

proved so brave and dar - ing, His fa - ther thought he'd ___
break - ers al - ways steer - ing, And I did not catch the ___
scope of this dis - as - ter, But I had - n't the face to re -

Copyright © 2004 by G. Schirmer, Inc. (ASCAP) New York, NY
International Copyright Secured. All Rights Reserved.

'pren - tice him to __ some ca - reer sea - far - ing. I __
word a - right, through _ be - ing hard of hear - ing. Mis -
turn to my place, and _ break it to my mas - ter. A __

was, a - las! his __ nurs - 'ry - maid, and _ so it fell to
tak - ing my in - struc - tions, which with - in my brain did
nurs - 'ry - maid is __ not a - fraid of __ what you peo - ple

my lot To take and bind the __ prom - is - ing boy ap -
gy - rate, I took and bound this __ prom - is - ing boy ap -
call work, So I made up my mind to __ go as a kind of pi -

pren - tice to a *pi - lot.* A life not bad for a
pren - tice to a *pi - rate.* A sad mis - take it ___
rat - i - cal maid - of - all - work. And that is how you __

p

WHERE THE MUSIC COMES FROM

Lee Hoiby
(b. 1926)

Copyright © 1990 by G. Schirmer, Inc. (ASCAP) New York, NY
International Copyright Secured. All Rights Reserved.

feel.

I want to

walk in the earth - ly gar - den, Far from cit - ies, far from

fear. I want to talk to the grow - ing gar - den, To the

* pronounced *day – vas* (nature spirits)

ABOUT THE ENHANCED CDs

In addition to piano accompaniments playable on both your CD player and computer, these enhanced CDs also include tempo adjustment software for computer use only. This software, known as Amazing Slow Downer, was originally created for use in pop music to allow singers and players the freedom to independently adjust both tempo and pitch elements. Because we believe there may be valuable educational use for these features in classical and theatre music, we have included this software as a tool for both the teacher and student. For quick and easy installation instructions of this software, please see below.

In recording a piano accompaniment we necessarily must choose one tempo. Our choice of tempo, phrasing, ritardandos, and dynamics is carefully considered. But by the nature of recording, it is only one option.

However, we encourage you to explore your own interpretive ideas, which may differ from our recordings. This new software feature allows you to adjust the tempo up and down without affecting the pitch. We recommend that this new tempo adjustment feature be used with care and insight. Ideally, you will be using these recorded accompaniments and Amazing Slow Downer for practice only.

The audio quality may be somewhat compromised when played through the Amazing Slow Downer. This compromise in quality will not be a factor in playing the CD audio track on a normal CD player or through another audio computer program.

INSTALLATION FROM DOWNLOAD:

For Windows (XP, Vista or 7):
1. Download and save the .zip file to your hard drive.
2. Extract the .zip file.
3. Open the "ASD Lite" folder.
4. Double-click "setup.exe" to run the installer and follow the on-screen instructions.

For Macintosh (OSX 10.4 and up):
1. Download and save the .dmg file to your hard drive.
2. Double-click the .dmg file to mount the "ASD Lite" volume.
3. Double-click the "ASD Lite" volume to see its contents.
4. Drag the "ASD Lite" application into the Application folder.

INSTALLATION FROM CD:

For Windows (XP, Vista or 7):
1. Load the CD-ROM into your CD-ROM drive.
2. Open your CD-ROM drive. You should see a folder named "Amazing Slow Downer." If you only see a list of tracks, you are looking at the audio portion of the disk and most likely do not have a multi-session capable CD-ROM.
3. Open the "Amazing Slow Downer" folder.
4. Double-click "setup.exe" to install the software from the CD-ROM to your hard disk. Follow the on-screen instructions to complete installation.
5. Go to "Start," "Programs" and find the "Amazing Slow Downer Lite" application. Note: To guarantee access to the CD-ROM drive, the user should be logged in as the "Administrator."

For Macintosh (OSX 10.4 or higher):
1. Load the CD-ROM into your CD-ROM drive.
2. Double-click on the data portion of the CD-ROM (which will have the Hal Leonard icon in red and be named as the book).
3. Open the "Amazing OSX" folder.
4. Double-click the "ASD Lite" application icon to run the software from the CD-ROM, or copy this file to your hard drive and run it from there.

MINIMUM SOFTWARE REQUIREMENTS:

For Windows (XP, Vista or 7):
Pentium Processor; Windows XP, Vista, or 7; 8 MB Application RAM; 8x Multi-Session CD-ROM drive

For Macintosh (OSX 10.4 or higher):
Power Macintosh or Intel Processor; Mac OSX 10.4 or higher; MB Application RAM; 8x Multi-Session CD-ROM drive